The Guinea Pig

Buying and Caring for your Pet

By Cindy Wright

Front Cover Photo:
In Loving Memory of
Tinkerbell 2008 – 2013

The Guinea Pig
Buying and Caring for your Pet

Cindy Wright

Copyright © 2013 by Cindy Wright.

To order additional copies of this book, contact:
Email: cindybooksuite@gmail.com
Website: http://theglobeuk.siterubix.com/

Contents

A Brief History of the Guinea Pig

A Brief History of the Guinea Pig

Before it became a household pet, the guinea pig, *Cavia Procellus*, or cuy, once lived in the wild.

The Domestication of the Guinea Pig

Researchers speculate that man began raising guinea pigs up to seven thousand years ago. This began when the little creatures were captured and the wild *Cavia Procellus* became livestock for farmers of the central Andes region of South American. Like other animals, such as wild dogs, wild cats and wild boars, the guinea pig's features and size changed once they became more domesticated.

Today many Andean farmers still keep guinea pigs, raising them as livestock. Domesticated cuys are kept inside buildings or stonewalled enclosures so they won't wander off. They are not always kept in cages, however. Some enjoy special rooms or cubbyholes inside the Andean family home. Most families keep twenty or so cuys, which provide the family with up to twelve pounds of meat a week. Because guinea pigs breed so rapidly and gain weight quickly on a diet that consists of barley, vegetables and Andean beer residue, they remain plentiful, providing families with enough meat.

South American Species: Imposter or Crossbreed?

Guinea pigs are called cuys in the Andes Mountain area of Southern America, because they reproduce quickly, they are a quick and steady meat source. South Americans have identified some twenty different species of the little creatures that are native to their country. But while these little animals may look and sound like the domesticated guinea pig, they are not the same species. The South America look-alike is skinnier than the domestic guinea pig. Moreover, studies have discovered that the South American guinea pig is supported by a different digestive system.

It is possible that we will never see the wild guinea pig. Its species, like the dinosaur, may have ceased to exist in the wild. Another hypothesis is that the wild guinea pig has morphed into an altered species to accommodate environmental differences and thus, no longer looks, sounds or behaves like the domestic guinea pig. A third hypothesis is that the guinea pig began breeding with other species and a new creature has evolved from natural crossbreeding.

Incan Livestock Travels to Europe

The first examples of domestication of the guinea pig occurred in the Inca tribe of Peru some five thousand years ago. Guinea pigs - or cavies as they were then known - were raised to become sacrificial animals to please the Inca gods. It makes sense that these animals were to be a diner fit for the gods, as special care was taken in the breeding to make them taste better.

Today, guinea pigs are still used as meat sources. In countries like Patagonia and Peru they are raised much the same as domestic pigs, cattle and chickens.

When the Europeans arrived in the sixteenth century to conquer the Incas, they fell in love with the cute little guinea pigs and scooped up several of them to take home with them. Guinea pigs were about to move from livestock to pets!

What's in a Name?

When the Europeans brought the cute creatures from Peru, they were not yet called guinea pigs. No one knows for sure how this endearing little fur ball got its present name; one can only speculate. One theory is that the guinea pig got its name from a port of call on the Europeans' way home from South America. Whether the guinea pig was named after New Guinea is pure speculation.

Another theory is that they were sold to the British for a guinea and hence the name was created.

Neither theory explains the other half of its name. It can't be the meat itself as my traveller friends who have sampled the meat insist that, like the wild rabbit and the alligator, roasted guinea pig "tastes just like chicken."

The best theory is that these little cavies made oinking noises that sounded closest to those of a pig. Germans called this new pet *Meerschweinschen*, which means "little pigs from across the sea".

And so, the cute little grunting and oinking creatures became known as guinea pigs, settling into a status as pets where they bred rapidly.

Guinea Pigs become Lab Rats

It is no accident when cooks tell their diners that they are using them as guinea pigs for a new recipe. By the early 1900's European scientists had discovered a new use for the guinea pig.

Like humans, guinea pigs cannot produce vitamin C. They too must get it from what they eat. In order to discovery remedies for a lack of vitamin C, guinea pigs became lab animals. Because of the guinea pig, mankind now enjoys medications for such diseases as: asthma, diphtheria and tuberculosis. Replacement valves for the human heart were developed and perfected because of research on guinea pigs.

Fast Forward to the 21st Century

In some parts of South America the guinea pig is still farmed as a source of meat. Guinea pig is a special dish for holidays such as: Easter, Carnival, Christmas and Corpus Christi. The popularity of this dish during special occasions is thought to be a throwback to the days of Inca sacrifices to their gods.

While some experimentation is still done using guinea pigs, they are not the lab animals of choice. Mice, rats, mayflies and monkeys have replaced guinea pigs in most labs for a variety of reasons.

Today, guinea pigs have a happier niche. Guinea pigs have become pampered pets in many Western homes. They are less work than cats and dogs, less expensive to purchase and look after, and much more convenient for households where both parents work outside the home.

The Wild Guinea Pig vs. the Domesticated Guinea Pig

Laboratory studies of the wild Andean cuys and modern-day tame guinea pigs have uncovered some interesting differences. These may have widespread application to the domestication of other animals throughout history. Both appearance and behaviour of the rodent now known as the guinea pig can be noted. Since both wild and domestic forms of guinea pigs can be studied in a laboratory, behavioural studies of the differences have been completed. Differences between wild and domestic guinea pigs are in some part behavioural; and part physical. The original wild cuys were smaller, drabber in appearance, have shorter hair and more vicious than the domesticated guinea pig. Where the domestic pet is gregarious, wild cuy males are loners. Wild cuys live in family groups called *harems*. Each harem has only one male and several females.

Tame guinea pigs live well in groups. They are content to have human touch and spend large periods of time grooming, as well as engaging in mating behaviour.

The Guinea Pig

Appearance

Modern domesticated adult guinea pigs make adorable pets. The guinea pig has a large head, short ears and chubby, stocky legs. The guinea pig's fat little body has only a stump of a tail. Originally a dull grey to blend into the environment, guinea pigs can now be purchased in black, brown, red and/or white.

A native of the Andes Mountains, the guinea pig is approximately ten inches long. It can weigh a pound or two. Once vicious creatures residing in one male harems, guinea pigs now live in domestic bliss, seemingly unconcerned about the ratio of males to females in their cages.

Guinea pigs have an excellent sense of smell, hearing and tactile sense but their eyesight is very poor.

There are nine species of *Cavia Porcellos* or Cavy. The male is called a boar, as in any pig family. The female is a sow, but baby guinea pigs are often referred to as pups rather than piglets.

Guinea Pig Reproduction

Guinea pigs usually give birth to three or four babies, called pups not piglets. Guinea pigs may have up to four litters in a year. If you are not breeding guinea pigs, be careful to keep adult and male pets separate or you will have a litter on your hands.

Habits

In the wild, cuys or undomesticated guinea pigs eat vegetation like grass. In the wild a harem or guinea pig family would live in a burrow or cave-like hole.

Whereas wild cuys or guinea pigs are nocturnal foragers to avoid predators, pet guinea pigs can adapt to the routines of the household. They will sleep all day if the household is quiet, but be ready for guinea pigs spinning on exercise wheels at night if they are allowed to sleep all day!

Diet

Guinea pigs usually live from five to seven years so they make great pets for children. Originally herbivores, guinea pigs like vegetables, grains and even table scraps. You can buy food especially mixed for your pet or create mixed grains and vegetable pieces for them.

Guinea Pigs as Pets

Because guinea pigs are small, furry and adorable, they make ideal pets for children. Guinea pigs don't take up much space. They are relatively safe pets as well, and they will not bite or scratch.

Guinea pigs recognise their owners and are delightful around children. Healthy guinea pigs are busy and bright-eyed; choose one of those for your child. Guinea pigs relate well to other guinea pigs and to people. When they are hungry, thirsty or just want to play, they let their owners know through special squeaks, whistles or cheeps. In no time your children will understand what their pet wants.

Getting Ready for your Pet

Your pet guinea pig needs a large cage because they like a lot of space. Purchase wood shavings or other bedding material that is clean and shredded.

The cage needs a bottle to hold fresh water. The food dish should be made of some material like ceramic, so it doesn't get tipped over while your pet is feeding. The guinea pig cage should also be equipped with a rack to hold fruit and vegetable pieces.

Guinea pigs like to have a hiding place where they feel safe. A piece of PVC pipe is perfect for your pet's sleeping/hiding space.

Guinea pigs, like humans, get their vitamin C from their food so make sure you buy food with added vitamin C or get vitamin C drops to add to your pet's food or water.

Guinea pigs will eat their own faeces. I know this seems weird but it is not unusual. Guinea pigs acquire more minerals and nutrients when their food is recycled.

Your pet's cage should be in a well-illuminated location, but not too close to the heat. Guinea pigs get heat stroke very easily. The cage should also be placed in a well-ventilated location away from draughts.

Guinea pigs are playful so they like toys in their cage. They will climb over them, push them around with their noses, and chew on them. The best toys for your pet's cage are natural wood ones that are safe to chew.

Clean your pet's cage at least once a week. Guinea pigs are neat and clean. They do not appreciate a filthy home.

Great Amusements and Diversions for Your Pet

Guinea pigs are very social so the very best diversion for your pet is another guinea pig. However, be very careful that they are not the same sex or guinea pups will overrun you in no time!

Hidey houses are great guinea pig diversions. Hidey houses and tunnels make your pet feel safe and snuggly. If you have two guinea pigs you need two hidey houses. That way there is no fighting.

Even though your pet has a large cage with toys and diversions he also needs out of the cage exercise.

Floor time should be away from appliances and furniture and enclosed spaces so your guinea pig does not escape or get hurt. Some people make an enclosure and others cover the floor of the bathtub with non-slip rugs or mats. Try to give your pet at least thirty minutes a day of floor time.

Lap time is a pleasant diversion for your guinea pig as well. Guinea pigs love to be patted and brushed, as well as held.

Guinea pigs love hay - whether in a mound in their cage or in a hayrack. They especially love fresh nice-smelling hay. Chewing it is good for their molars.

Beware of commercial pet toys. Cat balls with bells inside come apart leaving dangerous small pieces they can swallow. A good rule is the simpler the better. Some examples are washcloths set up as tents, paper bags, oatmeal containers, toilet paper and paper towel rolls and sheets of newspaper!

Guinea pigs love variety so change toys, houses and locations often. They even like changes in food dishes. Arrange toys and houses in the middle of the cage so there is a running track along the outside wall of the cage.

Grooming Your Guinea Pig

Making Sure Your Pet Guinea Pig is Properly Groomed

Guinea pigs are very tidy creatures. They hate grime and are happiest with a clean cage. Clean your pet's cage at least once a week. Fresh hay and shavings are needed to keep the cage clean. Since guinea pigs often "eat their food twice" by eating up the droppings, the cage needs to stay fairly clean and odour-free.

Your guinea pig will squeal and chirp with delight when he gets fresh wood shavings, a new toilet paper roll, fresh water and nice-smelling hay.

It is free entertainment for both you and your pet to watch him chew up newspaper or skitter in and out of his hidey house.

Guinea pigs make great pets because they are inexpensive, take up little space and require little care. Cats and dogs can bite and scratch, and dogs require walking. Guinea pigs' veterinary bills are not as great as a dog or a cat. A guinea pig is a great beginner pet to teach kids about the responsibility of pet care.

Brushing

One of the skills that children will develop while they are learning to raise their pet guinea pig is grooming. Like a dog, guinea pigs need regular brushing. Brushing your guinea pig keeps their coat in good condition.

Shorthaired guinea pigs do not shed as much or take as much grooming time. The hair doesn't mat or tangle as easily either.

Shorthaired: you really only need to brush short haired guinea pigs every few days or at least once a week. If they tend to shed then you should brush them every other day, if not every day.

Longhaired: For longhaired guinea pigs you need to take time every day to comb out any mats. If you have a hard time keeping up with grooming a longhaired guinea pig, than you can choose to trim its hair. Trim the longer hair so it's not dragging when they walk, or you can take them to a groomer to have their hair trimmed.

When you are brushing check for mites, lice or sores on their skin.

Guinea pig brushes should be soft like a baby's hairbrush, as your pet's skin is very delicate. You can purchase most guinea pig grooming supplies from pet shops and online suppliers.

Besides soft-bristled brushes specially designed for guinea pigs, you can get sprays that leave your pet and his cage smelling clean and fresh. Brush gently, and then comb.

Look for guinea pig grooming kits that include brushes as well as skin and coat supplements, which make your pet clean, healthy and happy.

Besides brushing your guinea pig, you should examine its eyes, ears and nose closely on a regular basis to ensure they are clean and don't contain debris. Use a warm, damp flannel to wipe away mucus from the corners of your pet's eyes.

Bathing

When bathing your guinea pig, use shampoo for small animals. Never use products designed for humans or other animals.

Guinea pigs groom themselves and rarely

require bathing unless they get covered with something. This is a good thing because guinea pigs don't like a bath. Bathing dries their skin. Male guinea pigs benefit from butt baths as that area can get messy.

The bath water should be lukewarm and lower than your guinea pig. Wet your pet, shampoo, rinse, and wrap in a warm towel to dry.

Tooth Brushing

Like dogs, guinea pigs need their teeth brushed. Buy guinea pig tooth paste from a pet store or vet. Take your pet out of his cage and put him on a towel on your lap. Squeeze toothpaste on a cloth and smear it on your pet's teeth. After you are finished gently scrubbing your guinea pig's teeth, keep him on your lap for fifteen minutes so the toothpaste soaks in.

Nail Clipping

If nails get long they become painful for your pet. Placing rocks, rough stones, bricks and other similar surfaces in their cages will help to wear their nails down so you won't need to clip them as often - if at all. Bricks are probably the cheapest, but make sure they are the solid types without any holes. There is too much of a risk of injury as their feet may get caught as they run over them.

You can have their nails done with a groomer or vet, but it is easy to do yourself - especially if their nails are light; just make sure to avoid the blood vessels. Get guinea pig nail cutters, hold your pet in your lap, pick a foot and choose a nail. Cut on an angle and only the end. If your pet is squeaking and wiggling you are cutting too close. Keep a styptic pen handy in case you cut too close to the vessel, which will stop the bleeding immediately.

Dispel the Smell!

There is no delicate way to put this; guinea pigs can smell. The scent of an unclean guinea pig cage is not nice. To solve this problem, clean the guinea pig's cage every day. Using a special cage odour control bedding like such as crumped paper with baking soda will dispel the odour in the cage. Guinea pigs don't smell if you keep their environment clean. Remove the soiled bedding daily. Once a week, clean it out fully. Use a vinegar and water solution in the cage to clear any urine smells.

You might also plug in a Febreeze pet scent odour eliminator in the wall near the cage.

Guinea Pig Health

Common Guinea Pig Diseases and Ailments

Luckily, guinea pigs do not get ill often. However, when they do get sick, it is almost always quite serious. A sick guinea pig's health will deteriorate rapidly. The first thing you may notice is a lack of appetite in your guinea pig; they will stop eating. If this occurs, get your guinea pig to an experienced vet, and don't wait around hoping he will improve; he won't!

The good news is, if illness is detected early, it can usually be cured fairly easily with antibiotics, which are safe for guinea pigs.

Warning Signs of a Sick Guinea Pig

- Refusal to eat or drink

- Any swollen areas on the body; these may be caused by injury, parasites, an abscess, a cyst or a tumour

- Panting, wheezing, or sneezing may be a sign of pneumonia or another other respiratory ailment

- Discharge from eyes, ears or nose; all of these three body parts should be clean and free of discharge

- Rough or matted fur

- Dull and/or sunken eyes

- Lethargy

- Pain; hunched over, flinches when touched or is sitting in an unusual position

- Drooling; drooling excessively, or if its teeth are sticking out of its mouth more than usual indicates dental problems or something caught in its throat

- Change in stools; a change in the colour or consistency of a guinea pig's droppings is a warning sign, stay aware of your guinea pig's bathroom behaviour

- Blood in urine

- Limping

- Hair loss can indicate skin disorders, parasites or fungal disorders

- Loss of balance

- Any behaviour that is unusual for your guinea pig

General Care

- Groom your pet daily

- Clean your guinea pig's cage at least once a week

- Provide fresh bedding and remove soiled bedding daily

- Make sure your pet has fresh water and that he is drinking it

- Make sure hay, vegetables and grains are fresh and that your pet is eating.

- Clean eyes with a damp wash cloth

- Remove debris from eyes, nose, mouth and ears gently with tweezers

You can monitor the health of your guinea pig by weighing him weekly. Two or three ounces of weight loss may indicate an illness. If your guinea pig has lost four or more ounces, consult a vet immediately. A guinea pig that is not eating is seriously ill and must be seen by a vet for treatment and must be hand-fed. Watch for signs of behavioural changes.

Do not allow your vet to prescribe Amoxicillin! If your pet is prescribed antibiotics, ask how quickly the medication should take effect. If your guinea pig does poorly on a particular antibiotic and stops eating, call your vet to have antibiotics changed.

Guinea Pig Illnesses

Digestive Disorders:

Digestive problems can be caused by infections, stomach ulcers, poor diet, or reaction to antibiotics. Guinea pigs are very sensitive to medications so their reaction to them must be monitored closely.

Eye Injuries/Disorders:

Guinea pigs can get poked in the eye by hay or wires or bedding; eyes can also be irritated by soiled bedding or cleaning chemicals. Use dust-free bedding. Make sure bedding is changed often and that there are no sharp objects in the cage. If your pet's eyes are dull or sunken see a vet. In addition to eye injuries, common eye disorders in guinea pigs are pink eye and cataracts. Seek medical advice if any of these occur.

C: Ears:

Guinea pig ears tend to get infections, become injured and attract parasites. If your pet is scratching excessively around his ears, is shaking and tilting its head or has a loss of balance, seek medical advice.

D: Heatstroke:

Guinea pigs take heatstroke very easily. Make sure the cage is in a well ventilated area out of direct light and that there is plenty of fresh water. Rapid breathing, drooling, lethargy and lack of balance are signs of heatstroke. To cool your guinea pig, place him in the sink in a couple of inches of cool water. Keep his head above water so he can breathe. Wrap a towel loosely for transport. Prevent heatstroke by checking to be sure the room temperature stays between 65 degrees and 75 degrees Fahrenheit.

E: Foot Problems:

Check for swollen, cracked or bleeding feet. This can be from nails cut too short or rough surfaces in the cage to keep nails short. If your pet is limping or its feet look red or swollen, take it to the vet.

F: Lumps:

In guinea pigs, lumps are usually caused by the streptococcus zooepidemicus bacterium. It makes a guinea pig look like they essentially have mumps. Swollen glands can become abscessed and may break open. Bacteria can travel throughout a guinea pig's body and can form abscesses in the internal organs, which can be fatal. These lumps are also contagious. Isolate infected guinea pigs from other pets. If your guinea pig develops lumps, your veterinarian may prescribe antibiotics.

G: Skin Problems:

If your guinea pig's coat is patchy, rough, sticking up, uneven or if baldness occurs on parts of its body, contact your vet. Some fungal skin infections can be passed to other pets and humans, so have your guinea pig's skin problems diagnosed and treated quickly.

H: Bites:

Guinea pigs do not bite on purpose. However, if their teeth are starting to grow too long, they may nip each other playfully. Bathe the bite area in antiseptic to keep the wound clean. If it becomes infected see a veterinarian.

I: Bloat:

Bloat is very serious. If your guinea pig has a rapid heart rate, breathing difficulties, no appetite, lethargy, constipation and an enlarged abdomen and seems in pain, seek veterinary assistance immediately.

J: Pneumonia:

Pneumonia is very common in guinea pigs, and results in death. Look for any coughing and sneezing. If any of these develop seek a veterinarian's help immediately.

K: Teeth:

A guinea pig's teeth carry on growing, and if they are not cared for properly can become overgrown. When this happens it can be very painful, causing the animal problems with eating. Always make sure there is plenty of hay, and chewable toys in their cage to help prevent this. If the problem is not fixed straight away, their teeth will begin to grow into the roof of the mouth or cheeks. Seek medical advice if this happens.

Choosing the Right Guinea Pig

Choosing a Guinea Pig Pet

Taking a lot of time to select the right pet may seem silly, but it is very worth it. You could go to the pet store and simply take home the one your child points out or accept one from a friend, but choosing the guinea pig that's right for you is not that simple. There are many things to be considered.

The important thing is to do the research first. Once your kids get involved you will look like the bad guy is you say no.

First of all consider this; do you have the right home and lifestyle for a guinea pig pet. Don't just choose a guinea pig because it seems like less work, cost and mess than a dog or a cat.

Ask yourself these questions:

1. Do you know cages require cleaning at least once a week - ideally every day?

2. Are you prepared to find an ideal space in your house with proper ventilation, free of draughts and at constant temperatures between 65 and 70 degrees?
3. How much are you prepared to spend to buy and house, feed and keep your guinea pig pet. Do you know what typical costs are?
4. Do you know if you want a male or a female?
5. Do you know the amount of time required to feed, water, clean and exercise your guinea pig daily?
6. Do you have someone to care for your pet reliably when you are away overnight or on holiday?
7. If you are committed to having a guinea pig, which breed do you feel is right for you? Why? Check the chapter on breeds before you choose.
8. Are you aware of guinea pig ailments and illnesses and the vet costs involved? Read the chapters on guinea pigs illness and parasites.

These are all questions you need to ask yourself seriously before buying a guinea pig.

Finding a Guinea Pig

Once you have decided a guinea pig is the pet for your household, then you need to think about where you are going to shop for your pet.

- Go to a pet store <u>only</u> if the staff is knowledgeable about guinea pigs, keep them in appropriate, clean housing, with a good diet and handle the guinea pigs regularly. Look for stores that house males and females separately, to avoid a surprise litter.

- Choose a guinea pig breeder. This is the best option - especially if you want a show quality pig or a specific breed. Breeders also keep good quality guinea pigs in a high quality environment. A good breeder will make sure the babies are socialised well and handled from an early age.

- Guinea pigs, sadly, often end up in shelters or rescue centres. This is a great place to give a guinea pig a second chance at life. Guinea pigs from shelters might be a little more skittish at first. They may not have been handled much when young. However, most of them settle down in their new homes once a routine is established and they get lots of cuddling and exercise time.

- Getting a guinea pig pet from a friend who has a litter of them is also a good way to provide a home for a guinea pig that might be sent to a shelter, drowned or may end up living in overcrowded conditions. You'd also be doing a favour for a friend. Maybe part of the agreement would be that your friend would pet sit if you were going to be away!

Whichever source is chosen, make sure the guinea pig appears in good health and condition, and is well socialised and easy to handle. Or you will have to be prepared to put in a lot of work with your new pet.

What to Look for When Choosing a Guinea Pig Pet

- Try to avoid guinea pigs that are panicky when handled, especially if they do not relax quickly, and also those that are overly quiet and calm. A too quiet or lethargic guinea pig may be sick.

- The guinea pig should be alert and active. That is normal behaviour for a guinea pig.

- Avoid guinea pigs that are too skinny or very overweight. The guinea pig's body is normally firm and rounded.

- Check the nose, eyes, ears and rear end to make sure there is no discharge.

- The guinea pig's coat should be full and soft - unless his breed is hairless or rough-coated.

- Check the skin for flakes or redness. These could be signs of parasites such as lice, mange mites or fleas. It is very hard to get rid of parasites once they have set in. If you have other rodent pets you do not want to take an infested animal home. Read the chapter on parasites.

Which Breed?

Your lifestyle and your personal interests have a lot to do with which breed of guinea pig you choose. For example, some may find hairless guinea pigs ugly but others think they are cute. Silkies are great guinea pigs if you are going to show them, but if you do not have the time this breed may not be suitable for you. Long haired pets can be cute, but the shedding and time spent grooming can be a deterrent. Teddys are the cutest and grooming time could be manageable. If you don't particularly want to get into costly vet bills choose one of the hardiest breeds with low grooming needs.

It's all a matter of what you want and what you have time for. Do the research first.

- Does your guinea pig need to be good with kids or are kids not present?
- Do you have specific colour or coat style preferences?
- Another consideration is where you are getting this pet? If you choose a breeder you have to choose one that breeds the guinea pig breed you are looking for. If you are going to a shelter, a pet shop or a friend you may have to be satisfied with what is available and you may be fine with that.
- If you are planning to show your pet, you need to be more careful when making a selection; a breeder is often the best way to go. Ask

others who show guinea pigs about what to look for.

A great way to get some input is to research the strength of each breed and the drawbacks of each and then make your decision.

For example, if you are tight on time for grooming and hate loose and shedding hair on you and in your house, but prefer a long-haired, generally good all round guinea pig pet, then a good choice is:

A Coronet:

Coronets are a bit like crested guinea pigs in appearance, except their coats are far longer. They have quite a lot of fur around the shoulders. To maintain an attractive and elegant coat you must regularly groom your guinea pig, as well as occasionally giving it a bath.

If on the other hand, you prefer a shorthaired guinea pig that is great with kids and you have the time for grooming and you don't mind shedding hair, but prefer a multi-coloured pet, then a perfect choice for you is the Crested guinea pig.

Crested guinea pigs have one rosette on the top of their heads, called a crown. There are two types of crested guinea pig; English and American. The English crest is the same colour as the rest of the coat. The American crest is pure white. Crested guinea pigs make wonderful pets if you don't mind finding lots of little hairs on your clothes and around your house. They are worth the vacuuming inconvenience.

Spending time finding out about the care and feeding of your future pet, as well as selecting the criteria for choosing the best pet for you is all part of the fun of pet ownership. Remember, getting there is part of the fun of taking a trip.

Guinea Pig Adaptations

Early Adaptations

Like most creatures, the guinea pig has managed to make several adaptations. First the guinea pig was a wild animal, but when it was time, the guinea pig had to adjust to domestication. Guinea pigs lived in the wild in South America in the Andes Mountains where the Incan people hunted them for food.

Gradually the Incas began to keep a few for food and raised the rest of them - often in part of their house. When the Europeans arrived in South America, they spied the cute little creatures and took them home to Europe as pets. Those guinea pigs had to adapt from being wild animals, to livestock and eventually to pets, as well as adapting to a climate change from South America to Europe.

Social Animals

Guinea pigs are highly social animals. They were easily able to adapt to domestication and becoming pets. Guinea pigs don't adapt well to life alone however, a single guinea pig as a pet is not a happy creature unless it has a lot of human companionship.

Adapting for Safety

When threatened by a predator, guinea pigs respond in one of three ways. They may remain still like a rabbit or possum until the threat is gone. If the guinea pigs are in a group, they will scatter in order to throw the predator off his stalking. Guinea pigs may also choose to flee. They are fast and they often have escape routes set up to allow them ground cover and hidey holes.

Natural Adaptations

Guinea pigs are equipped with many natural adaptations. Their sensory adaptations really help guinea pigs to protect themselves. Guinea pigs have excellent hearing, much better than a human. Guinea pigs like dogs, hear at higher frequencies than humans. They can hear a predator, and identify whether it is a danger to them. Guinea pigs also have a keen sense of smell. Other rodents like hamsters, mice and gerbils do not have as a sense of smell that is as well developed.

Guinea pigs have colour vision, which is unusual in rodents. Their depth perception is very poor so they use smell, taste and hearing to compensate.

The hairs on a guinea pigs' muzzle switch and detect vibrations in the air. Because their vision is poor, it helps them navigate. Since wild guinea pigs are nocturnal, well-developed sense of smell, touch and hearing are good senses to have.

Living Adaptations

The guinea pig's natural personality is amiable and shy, it was either to adapt to the wild or become another animal's dinner. Guinea pigs create a "safety net" by laying down twigs and branches. Wild guinea pigs will also create warrens and pathways through which guinea pigs can scramble to avoid predators like owls and hawks. The guinea pig developed intricate labyrinths to evade enemies.

Defensive Adaptations

When they are cornered, guinea pigs will put up a fight. They use their teeth to chew or bite their attacker.

Guinea pig's teeth are part of its adaptation. They grow constantly and are a source of protection and a vehicle for feeding. In order to keep teeth from becoming too long, the guinea pig gnaws on hay, cardboard and wood.

Survival Adaptations

Because the guinea pig can reproduce young and so frequently, they can avoid extinction. Even though the guinea pig has many predators and is a peaceful animal, they do what they have to in order to survive. His rapid reproduction rate and the fact that he is such an amiable, cute, little pet will always be in his favour.

The Lifespan of Your Guinea Pig

Guinea Pig Life Span

Cavies, or guinea pigs, will likely live for four to eight years. Six is an average life span but many guinea pigs live to be over ten! Your guinea pig will live longer if he is well cared for and well fed. Keeping them well-nourished and consulting with a vet regularly is a good way to extend your pet's life span.

Guinea pigs are not as hardy as you might think, (consult the chapter on illness for signs to watch out for). Illness can be difficult to detect in these pets. A guinea pig will often hide it's sickness until it gets too serious to treat, an inbred instinct. In the wild, guinea pigs hide from predators to avoid drawing attention.

Even the most experienced owners can miss signs of sickness. A good way to check the health of your pet is to keep track of his weight and behaviour. Look for changes in eating, drinking, activity, going to the bathroom, avoidance of being handled, etc. If something doesn't seem right, it is best to get to the vet right away. Guinea pig health can deteriorate fast.

During their lives guinea pigs pass through several stages:

1. Birth

Pregnancy lasts about sixty-eight days. Guinea pigs give birth to, on average, two to three young per litter. New-born pups each weigh about a few ounces to a pound. If a female guinea pig does not breed before six months of age, her pubic bones may fuse, preventing her from giving birth. About 20 per cent of guinea sows die in delivery. Litters should be separated, to give the mother time to recuperate, (see chapter on breeding for more details).

2. Pup Stage

Guinea pig pups are precocial. They are born fully furred, with well-developed sensory and locomotor abilities, and they can consume solid food the same day they are born. Pups can be weaned after five days, but they normally nurse for three weeks or more. Milk consumption decreases as solid food consumption increases. The mother grooms her young very little.

Well-developed young pups have high-energy needs right after birth. However, the pup's milk consumption decreases rapidly, and so daily maternal energy expenditure decreases also. This strategy may enable guinea pigs to breed throughout the year.

3. Mature Guinea Pigs

Females reach sexual maturity at two months of age. Males reach it at three months. Pet guinea pigs usually live five to seven years - sometimes as much as ten - if given proper care. During that time they can give birth to huge numbers of pups, (see chapter on breeding and "Pigs is Pigs" chapter for more information).

Pigs Is Pigs (A Short Story)
Ellis Parker Butler

Mike Flannery, the Westcote agent of the Interurban Express Company, leaned over the counter of the express office and shook his fist. Mr. Morehouse, angry and red, stood on the other side of the counter, trembling with rage. The argument had been long and heated, and at last Mr. Morehouse had talked himself speechless. The cause of the trouble stood on the counter between the two men. It was a soap box across the top of which were nailed a number of strips, forming a rough but serviceable cage. In it two spotted guinea-pigs were greedily eating lettuce leaves.

"Do as you loike, then!" shouted Flannery, "pay for thim an' take thim, or don't pay for thim and leave thim be. Rules is rules, Misther Morehouse, an' Mike Flannery's not goin' to be called down fer breakin' of thim."

"But, you everlastingly stupid idiot!" shouted Mr. Morehouse, madly shaking a flimsy printed book beneath the agent's nose, "can't you read it here-in your own plain printed rates? 'Pets, domestic, Franklin to Westcote, if properly boxed, twenty-five cents each.'" He threw the book on the counter in disgust. "What more do you want? Aren't they pets? Aren't they domestic? Aren't they properly boxed? What?"

He turned and walked back and forth rapidly; frowning ferociously.

Suddenly he turned to Flannery, and forcing his voice to an artificial calmness spoke slowly but with intense sarcasm.

"Pets," he said "P-e-t-s! Twenty-five cents each. There are two of them. One! Two! Two times twenty-five are fifty! Can you understand that? I offer you fifty cents."

Flannery reached for the book. He ran his hand through the pages and stopped at page sixty four.

"An' I don't take fifty cints," he whispered in mockery. "Here's the rule for ut. 'Whin the agint be in anny doubt regardin' which of two rates applies to a shipment, he shall charge the larger. The con-sign-ey may file a claim for the overcharge.' In this case, Misther Morehouse, I be in doubt. Pets thim animals may be, an' domestic they be, but pigs I'm blame sure they do be, an' me rules says plain as the nose on yer face, 'Pigs Franklin to Westcote, thirty cints each.' An' Mister Morehouse, by me arithmetical knowledge two times thurty comes to sixty cints."

Mr. Morehouse shook his head savagely. "Nonsense!" he shouted, "Confounded nonsense, I tell you! Why, you poor ignorant foreigner, that rule means common pigs, domestic pigs, not guinea pigs!"

Flannery was stubborn.

"Pigs is pigs," he declared firmly. "Guinea-pigs, or dago pigs or Irish pigs is all the same to the Interurban Express Company an' to Mike Flannery. Th' nationality of the pig creates no differentiality in the rate, Misther Morehouse! 'Twould be the same was they Dutch pigs or Rooshun pigs. Mike Flannery," he added, "is here to tind to the expriss business and not to hould conversation wid dago pigs in sivinteen languages fer to discover be they Chinese or Tipperary by birth an' nativity."

Mr. Morehouse hesitated. He bit his lip and then flung out his arms wildly.

"Very well!" he shouted, "you shall hear of this! Your president shall hear of this! It is an outrage! I have offered you fifty cents. You refuse it! Keep the pigs until you are ready to take the fifty cents, but, by

George, sir, if one hair of those pigs' heads is harmed I will have the law on you!"

He turned and stalked out, slamming the door. Flannery carefully lifted the soap box from the counter and placed it in a corner. He was not worried. He felt the peace that comes to a faithful servant who has done his duty and done it well.

Mr. Morehouse went home raging. His boy, who had been awaiting the guinea-pigs, knew better than to ask him for them. He was a normal boy and therefore always had a guilty conscience when his father was angry. So the boy slipped quietly around the house. There is nothing so soothing to a guilty conscience as to be out of the path of the avenger. Mr. Morehouse stormed into the house. "Where's the ink?" he shouted at his wife as soon as his foot was across the doorsill.

Mrs. Morehouse jumped, guiltily. She never used ink. She had not seen the ink, nor moved the ink, nor thought of the ink, but her husband's tone convicted her of the guilt of having borne and reared a boy, and she knew that whenever her husband wanted anything in a loud voice the boy had been at it.

"I'll find Sammy," she said meekly.

When the ink was found Mr. Morehouse wrote rapidly, and he read the completed letter and smiled a triumphant smile.

"That will settle that crazy Irishman!" he exclaimed. "When they get that letter he will hunt another job, all right!"

A week later Mr. Morehouse received a long official envelope with the card of the Interurban Express Company in the upper left corner. He tore it open eagerly and drew out a sheet of paper. At the top it bore the number A6754. The letter was short. "Subject--Rate on guinea-pigs," it said, "Dr. Sir--We are in receipt of your letter regarding rate on guinea-pigs between Franklin and Westcote addressed to the president of this company. All claims for overcharge should be addressed to the Claims Department."

Mr. Morehouse wrote to the Claims Department. He wrote six pages of choice sarcasm, vituperation and argument, and sent them to the Claims Department.

A few weeks later he received a reply from the Claims Department. Attached to it was his last letter.

"Dr. Sir," said the reply. "Your letter of the 16th inst., addressed to this Department, subject rate on guinea-pigs from Franklin to Westcote, rec'd. We have taken up the matter with our agent at Westcote, and his reply is attached herewith. He informs us that you refused to receive the consignment or to pay the charges. You have therefore no claim against this company, and your letter regarding the proper rate on the consignment should be addressed to our Tariff Department."

Mr. Morehouse wrote to the Tariff Department. He stated his case clearly, and gave his arguments in full, quoting a page or two from the encyclopaedia to prove that guinea-pigs were not common pigs.

With the care that characterizes corporations when they are systematically conducted, Mr. Morehouse's letter was numbered, O.K'd, and started through the regular channels. Duplicate copies of the bill of lading, manifest, Flannery's receipt for the package and several other pertinent papers were pinned to the letter, and they were passed to the head of the Tariff Department.

The head of the Tariff Department put his feet on his desk and yawned. He looked through the papers carelessly.

"Miss Kane," he said to his stenographer, "take this letter. 'Agent, Westcote, N. J.

Please advise why consignment referred to in attached papers was refused domestic pet rates."'

Miss Kane made a series of curves and angles on her note book and waited with pencil poised. The head of the department looked at the papers again.

"Huh! guinea-pigs!" he said. "Probably starved to death by this time! Add this to that letter: 'Give condition of consignment at present.'"

He tossed the papers on to the stenographer's desk, took his feet from his own desk and went out to lunch.

When Mike Flannery received the letter he scratched his head.

"Give prisint condition," he repeated thoughtfully. "Now what do thim clerks be wantin' to know, I wonder! Prisint condition, 'is ut? Thim pigs, praise St. Patrick, do be in good health, so far as I know, but I niver was no veternairy surgeon to dago pigs. Mebby thim clerks wants me to call in the pig docther an' have their pulses took. Wan thing I do know, howiver, which is they've glorious appytites for pigs of their soize. Ate? They'd ate the brass padlocks off of a barn door I If the paddy pig, by the same token,

63

ate as hearty as these dago pigs do, there'd be a famine in Ireland."

To assure himself that his report would be up to date, Flannery went to the rear of the office and looked into the cage. The pigs had been transferred to a larger box-- a dry goods box.

"Wan, -- two, -- t'ree, -- four, -- five, -- six, -- sivin, -- eight!" he counted. "Sivin spotted an' wan all black. All well an' hearty an' all eatin' loike ragin' hippypottymusses. He went back to his desk and wrote.

"Mr. Morgan, Head of Tariff Department," he wrote. "Why do I say dago pigs is pigs because they is pigs and will be til you say they ain't which is what the rule book says stop your jollying me you know it as well as I do. As to health they are all well and hoping you are the same. P. S. There are eight now the family increased all good eaters. P. S. I paid out so far two dollars for cabbage which they like shall I put in bill for same what?"

Morgan, head of the Tariff Department, when he received this letter, laughed. He read it again and became serious.

"By George!" he said, "Flannery is right, 'pigs is pigs.' I'll have to get authority on this thing. Meanwhile, Miss Kane, take this letter: Agent, Westcote, N. J. Regarding shipment guinea-pigs, File No. A6754. Rule 83, General Instruction to Agents, clearly states that agents shall collect from consignee all costs of provender, etc., etc., required for livestock while in transit or storage. You will proceed to collect same from consignee."

Flannery received this letter next morning, and when he read it he grinned.

"Proceed to collect," he said softly. "How thim clerks do loike to be talkin'! I proceed to collect two dollars and twinty-foive cints off Misther Morehouse! I wonder do thim clerks know Misther Morehouse. I'll git it! Oh, yes! 'Misther Morehouse, two an' a quarter, plaze.' 'Cert'nly, me dear frind Flannery. Delighted!' Not!"

Flannery drove the express wagon to Mr. Morehouse's door. Mr. Morehouse answered the bell.

"Ah, ha!" he cried as soon as he saw it was Flannery. "So you've come to your senses at last, have you? I thought you would! Bring the box in."

"I hev no box," said Flannery coldly. "I hev a bill agin Misther John C. Morehouse for two dollars and twinty-foive cints for

kebbages aten by his dago pigs. Wud you
wish to pay ut?"

"Pay--Cabbages--!" gasped Mr. Morehouse.
"Do you mean to say that two little guinea-
pigs--"

"Eight!" said Flannery. "Papa an' mamma
an' the six childer. Eight!"

For answer Mr. Morehouse slammed the
door in Flannery's face. Flannery looked at
the door reproachfully.

"I take ut the con-sign-y don't want to pay
for thim kebbages," he said. "If I know
signs of refusal, the con-sign-y refuses to
pay for wan dang kebbage leaf an' be
hanged to me!"

Mr. Morgan, the head of the Tariff
Department, consulted the president of
the Interurban Express Company
regarding guinea-pigs, as to whether they
were pigs or not pigs. The president was
inclined to treat the matter lightly.

"What is the rate on pigs and on pets?" he
asked.

"Pigs thirty cents, pets twenty-five," said
Morgan.

"Then of course guinea-pigs are pigs," said the president.

"Yes," agreed Morgan, "I look at it that way, too. A thing that can come under two rates is naturally due to be classed as the higher. But are guinea-pigs, pigs? Aren't they rabbits?"

"Come to think of it," said the president, "I believe they are more like rabbits. Sort of half-way station between pig and rabbit. I think the question is this--are guinea-pigs of the domestic pig family? I'll ask Professor Gordon. He is authority on such things. Leave the papers with me."

The president put the papers on his desk and wrote a letter to Professor Gordon. Unfortunately the Professor was in South America collecting zoological specimens, and the letter was forwarded to him by his wife. As the Professor was in the highest Andes, where no white man had ever penetrated, the letter was many months in reaching him. The president forgot the guinea-pigs, Morgan forgot them, Mr. Morehouse forgot them, but Flannery did not. One-half of his time he gave to the duties of his agency; the other half was devoted to the guinea-pigs. Long before Professor Gordon received the president's letter Morgan received one from Flannery.

"About them dago pigs," it said, "what shall I do they are great in family life, no race suicide for them, there are thirty-two now shall I sell them do you take this express office for a menagerie, answer quick."

Morgan reached for a telegraph blank and wrote:

"Agent, Westcote. Don't sell pigs."

He then wrote Flannery a letter calling his attention to the fact that the pigs were not the property of the company but were merely being held during a settlement of a dispute regarding rates. He advised Flannery to take the best possible care of them.

Flannery, letter in hand, looked at the pigs and sighed. The dry-goods box cage had become too small. He boarded up twenty feet of the rear of the express office to make a large and airy home for them, and went about his business. He worked with feverish intensity when out on his rounds, for the pigs required attention and took most of his time. Some months later, in desperation, he seized a sheet of paper and wrote "160" across it and mailed it to Morgan. Morgan returned it asking for explanation. Flannery replied:

"There be now one hundred sixty of them dago pigs, for heaven's sake let me sell off some, do you want me to go crazy, what."

"Sell no pigs," Morgan wired.

Not long after this the president of the express company received a letter from Professor Gordon. It was a long and scholarly letter, but the point was that the guinea-pig was the Cava aparoea while the common pig was the genius Sus of the family Suidae. He remarked that they were prolific and multiplied rapidly.

"They are not pigs," said the president, decidedly, to Morgan. "The twenty-five cent rate applies."

Morgan made the proper notation on the papers that had accumulated in File A6754, and turned them over to the Audit Department. The Audit Department took some time to look the matter up, and after the usual delay wrote Flannery that as he had on hand one hundred and sixty guinea-pigs, the property of consignee, he should deliver them and collect charges at the rate of twenty-five cents each.

Flannery spent a day herding his charges through a narrow opening in their cage so that he might count them.

"Audit Dept." he wrote, when he had finished the count, "you are way off there may be was one hundred and sixty dago pigs once, but wake up don't be a back number. I've got even eight hundred, now shall I collect for eight hundred or what, how about sixty-four dollars I paid out for cabbages."

It required a great many letters back and forth before the Audit Department was able to understand why the error had been made of billing one hundred and sixty instead of eight hundred, and still more time for it to get the meaning of the "cabbages."

Flannery was crowded into a few feet at the extreme front of the office. The pigs had all the rest of the room and two boys were employed constantly attending to them. The day after Flannery had counted the guinea-pigs there were eight more added to his drove, and by the time the Audit Department gave him authority to collect for eight hundred Flannery had given up all attempts to attend to the receipt or the delivery of goods. He was hastily building galleries around the express office, tier above tier. He had four thousand and sixty-four guinea-pigs to care for! More were arriving daily.

Immediately following its authorization the Audit Department sent another letter, but Flannery was too busy to open it. They wrote another and then they telegraphed:

"Error in guinea-pig bill. Collect for two guinea-pigs, fifty cents. Deliver all to consignee."

Flannery read the telegram and cheered up. He wrote out a bill as rapidly as his pencil could travel over paper and ran all the way to the Morehouse home. At the gate he stopped suddenly. The house stared at him with vacant eyes. The windows were bare of curtains and he could see into the empty rooms. A sign on the porch said, "To Let." Mr. Morehouse had moved! Flannery ran all the way back to the express office. Sixty-nine guinea-pigs had been born during his absence. He ran out again and made feverish inquiries in the village. Mr. Morehouse had not only moved, but he had left Westcote. Flannery returned to the express office and found that two hundred and six guinea-pigs had entered the world since he left it. He wrote a telegram to the Audit Department.

"Can't collect fifty cents for two dago pigs consignee has left town address unknown what shall I do? Flannery."

The telegram was handed to one of the clerks in the Audit Department, and as he read it he laughed.

"Flannery must be crazy. He ought to know that the thing to do is to return the consignment here," said the clerk. He telegraphed Flannery to send the pigs to the main office of the company at Franklin.

When Flannery received the telegram he set to work. The six boys he had engaged to help him also set to work. They worked with the haste of desperate men, making cages out of soap boxes, cracker boxes, and all kinds of boxes, and as fast as the cages were completed they filled them with guinea-pigs and expressed them to Franklin. Day after day the cages of Guinea pigs flowed in a steady stream from Westcote to Franklin, and still Flannery and his six helpers ripped and nailed and packed--relentlessly and feverishly. At the end of the week they had shipped two hundred and eighty cases of guinea-pigs, and there were in the express office seven hundred and four more pigs than when they began packing them.

"Stop sending pigs. Warehouse full," came a telegram to Flannery. He stopped packing only long enough to wire back, "Can't stop," and kept on sending them.

On the next train up from Franklin came one of the company's inspectors. He had instructions to stop the stream of guinea-pigs at all hazards. As his train drew up at Westcote station he saw a cattle car standing on the express company's siding. When he reached the express office he saw the express wagon backed up to the door. Six boys were carrying bushel baskets full of guinea-pigs from the office and dumping them into the wagon. Inside the room Flannery, with' his coat and vest off, was shovelling guinea-pigs into bushel baskets with a coal scoop. He was winding up the guinea-pig episode.

He looked up at the inspector with a snort of anger.

"Wan wagonload more an, I'll be quit of thim, an' niver will ye catch Flannery wid no more foreign pigs on his hands. No, sur! They near was the death o' me. Nixt toime I'll know that pigs of whaiver nationality is domistic pets--an' go at the lowest rate."

He began shoveling again rapidly, speaking quickly between breaths.

"Rules may be rules, but you can't fool Mike Flannery twice wid the same thrick-- whin ut comes to live stock, dang the rules. So long as Flannery runs this expriss office--pigs is pets--an' cows is pets--an' horses is pets--an' lions an' tigers an' Rocky Mountain goats is pets--an' the rate on thim is twinty-foive cints."

He paused long enough to let one of the boys put an empty basket in the place of the one he had just filled. There were only a few guinea-pigs left. As he noted their limited number his natural habit of looking on the bright side returned.

"Well, annyhow," he said cheerfully, "'tis not so bad as ut might be. What if thim dago pigs had been elephants!"

Ellis Parker Butler's short story: "Pigs Is Pigs"